The Temporary Vase of Hands

poems by

Sandra Fees

Finishing Line Press
Georgetown, Kentucky

The Temporary Vase of Hands

Copyright © 2017 by Sandra Fees
ISBN 978-1-63534-158-4 First Edition
All rights reserved under International and Pan-American Copyright Conventions. No part of this book may be reproduced in any manner whatsoever without written permission from the publisher, except in the case of brief quotations embodied in critical articles and reviews.

ACKNOWLEDGMENTS

My sincere thanks to the editors and publications in which the following poems first appeared, sometimes in earlier versions:

Broad! (a gentleperson's magazine): "One Sock, Never Two" and "Scent of Brown Sugar and Fig"
FootHills Publishing Birdsong Anthology: "Wild Articulation"
Grit, Gravity and Grace (College of Physicians of Philadelphia): "Dementia Dreams"
New Madrid: "Fist of Winter" and "By Subtraction"
Right Hand Pointing: "The Sound Is Something Curving"
Rust+Moth: "Ruth"
Toasted Cheese: "Negative Space" and "Stats for the Living"
Touch: A Journal of Healing: "The Arc Horses Make"
Wilda Morris Poetry Blog: "The Sloping Room"
Wilderness House Literary Review: "Sleep's Indigo"

Publisher: Leah Maines

Editor: Christen Kincaid

Cover Art: Sandra Fees

Author Photo: Melissa Medina

Cover Design: Elizabeth Maines

Printed in the USA on acid-free paper.
Order online: www.finishinglinepress.com
　　　　　also available on amazon.com

Author inquiries and mail orders:
Finishing Line Press
P. O. Box 1626
Georgetown, Kentucky 40324
U. S. A.

Table of Contents

Indigenous 1
Sleep's Indigo 2
One Sock, Never Two 3
Afternoon Vignette 5
The Sound Is Something Curving 6
Scent of Brown Sugar and Fig 7
By Subtraction 8
Fist of Winter 9
Last Sprig 10
Stats for the Living 11
The Covenant 12
Negative Space 13
Ruth 14
The Sloping Room 15
The Arc Horses Make 16
Dementia Dreams 17
Johnny Red 19
Amplification 21
Treatise 22
Consignment Pockets 23
Pressed Close to the Secrets of Water 24
Temporary Vase 25
Whispered Season 26
Wild Articulation 27

in memory of my parents
Ruth Ella Kanode Fees and John Darkes Fees

Indigenous

River birch
Pennsylvania native

split trunk and peeling bark
speaks of death

tells me what I already know:
Everything you love will fall apart.

Stationary sycamore
resolute elder

grown solid with endurance
speaks of life

tells me what I already know:
Nothing you love will ever be lost.

Sleep's Indigo

Just as expected, Pennsylvania's Blue Mountains
stretch behind farmer Smith's field.

Mother reclines in a *Woman's Day* magazine,
dipping and rising in sleep's indigo print.

Her dreams survey the back roads
from home to somewhere she will never get to.

A creased map spreads out in her lap.
She always had a poor sense of direction.

This in-between land becomes
a garment she learns to wear,

more like evening than armor
as she plots the route between worlds.

One Sock, Never Two

Separating from the only skin
I'll ever grow inside
besides my own: *Mother ...*

I learn to leave things behind—
parts of myself and other people—
sometimes without wanting to
but not always.

This is how it is
to back out of a familiar driveway
one last time. You think you are ready.

Or to sing *amazing grace*
by my dying mother's bedside
but to feel no mercy
as I slip for the second time in my life
from her body on a hospital cot
scrunched like a newborn.

All our lives we are losing things
and by degrees—
zest, fingernails, mooring, the gods,
a set of keys, a way of life, a time zone,
one sock, never two.

We lose ourselves and each other
at least once sometimes twice
maybe more before it's done.

Someone tells me we're better off
without our attachments
though no one seems entirely sure.

The glint in another's eyes
reflects what I wanted to know all along
something of inherent being.

Love's unknowns
call for bodily reunion
and brew deep in earth.

Afternoon Vignette

Sun catches in sky's collarbone
like a topaz pendant,
our final afternoons
an extended motion of hands.

We paint ancient circles
in sapphire, garnet, and jade,
dangling as close to happiness
as we dare to get.

The Sound Is Something Curving

The years string eighty-eight
shards of light around her neck.
Are they skulls or prayer beads?

When the knot loosens, they scatter
striking floor tiles like tiny mallets.
The sound is something curving

like the bowl of the body, all crescents
and clinging, cheated of last embraces
refracting the harmonics of regret.

Scent of Brown Sugar and Fig

You draw yourself close.
Yes, a moth.

So close you can feel heat
still rising from the chest

like a flame faltering
in its final moments.

If you come still closer
there's a scent of food—

brown sugar
and fig.

But it's only Mother's lotion
the body's last preparation

its last longing for human hands
to linger on the skin.

Shadows crowd the light
in the window.

By Subtraction

Three animals in one year
come in snow to die. Here. Why?

Sirens invade the housing project
across the bridge.

The sky turns pale pink,
the way it does when it snows. Light pollution.

A lone rabbit, more scared than me,
loses the familiar earth-scent

can't get comfortable
in winter's skin.

Mother's final message replays:
I just called to see if you're all snowed in

her voice tripping a little over the words *snowed in*
as if telling a half-joke.

Before that, I thought I knew what I wanted to say.
Now it's her voice I hear.

Some people believe when a person dies
they take part of you with them. But it isn't true.

They leave part behind
and what they leave isn't yours to keep.

By subtraction, you'll leave still more,
each moment another shade of white.

Fist of Winter

The end begins this way:

bees exit the hive
without fear or regret.

A brown heart remains
suspended in magnolia's branches.

The urge to take a stick
and swat it down like a piñata
prickles my skin with the certainty
it can't last the season.

Blizzard sets the dark pendulum free
like a house built for abandon
and demolition.

Wading into knee-deep snow,
I cup hive to hands,

the human heart
gripped in winter's fist.

Last Sprig

When I'm an old woman,
I'll snip a sprig of bleeding heart
and guide it into a bud vase.

I'll feel night's whisker
against my cheek
and sit cross-legged

like a young girl waiting.
I'll remember the first place
I lived and the last,

the first moment my eyes
greeted my mother's gaze
and the last hours of grace.

Stats for the Living
after Yehuda Amichai

For every person in a hurry to die,
there are three to pull her back.

For the dying who can't die,
the living to push them through
and the dead cajoling.

For the weary,
plenty of shoulders.

For the lonely,
those who will take their money.

For morning people,
the unrelenting hunger of goldfinches

and garbage trucks rattling up and down streets
with unwanted tins and wrappers
that can't breathe or stop breathing.

For evening people,
there is the memory
of what no longer loves
but can still be loved.

    And there is sleep,
crowded by cicadas,

by dreaming
and you.

The Covenant

Late afternoon houses
turn blue as the hillside.

Tattered sweaters hang from clotheslines
like prayer flags

but no peace descends.
Far from home,

sequestering myself on this rooftop,
I peer below where women,

gnarled with age,
traverse the cobbled street.

The cadence of voices drifts upward
only half-heard half-understood

and the sky is burnished
with uncertain promises.

Negative Space

When sand is so hot on the feet
you forget how to walk

and when prayer is the shape
of a teacup

Because the young woman tells her boyfriend:
negative space is cool

and because the room is too big
and the world too small

After you drink holy water
in the Narayan temple

and sacrifice what was
for what is

Then everywhere is a tree
wanting to be climbed

and everywhere arms press
into sleeves of air.

Ruth

My father fixes his glazed eyes on the splintered
horizon where old farmer Smith's blade sheared

rows of cornstalks into tiny syllables, baring the field's
belly, delineating its expansions and contractions.

Beyond that, mountains stoop silently on blue
knees in distant devotion as if expecting guests

to pause roadside, seeking communion with the past.
My gaze rests on the farmhouse, to the corner

that was once my bedroom, which slants, just
enough for a marble to roll evenly, one side

to the other, without the tiniest push.
I startle as a car approaches from behind, shifts

abruptly into the oncoming lane, speeds by. A bird,
probably a swallow, angles overhead with conviction,

scrawling its whole self across sky. I say my mother's
name. Beside me in the passenger seat, my father

half-echoes: *my wife's name was Ruth.*
Her name framed by his lips, a credential in danger

of losing its relevance, he asks:
how old are you?

I press my memory against something I can't name,
cool and rooted. *I am 52. My middle name is Ruth.*

The Sloping Room

When he pulled down
the rotted porch
my father discovered
why the front bedroom
sloped as it did
not from settling after all
or from the gremlins
roiling under my bed

but because a log
was missing
as if in building
there were some hurry
or a timber shortage
as if the poor man's farmhouse
would naturally lean a little
deserve a little less

to keep him honest
and always on bended knee
just the way my father taught me
to bend my knees
toward the rough planks
to press palm to palm
my small body
a pew wanting to be a steeple

a 90-degree angle
forming squares and quadrangles
when all I really wanted
were hula hoops
to swing around my hips
and little wheels
to spin their o's
in the sloping room.

The Arc Horses Make

All history in the end,
my father says,

looking straight ahead at the photograph
propped on the roll-top desk,

he and Bye Bye Shadow in the spotlight,
my mother just beyond the camera's reach.

No one bothers to discard the maroon
and gold racing suit he wore
that night in the winner's circle.

It hangs in the closet absent the helmet,
which exists now only on film.

Life fans out behind him
like the arc horses make in the home stretch.

I miss you, he says,
when I rise to leave,

and he means what crossed the finish
that once kept us warm.

It is flesh he misses,
heat escalating off flanks
and taut sinews,

two pacing as one.

Dementia Dreams

If his slender room,
were all I could see,

this crank-handled window,
and beyond it,
this moment groaning toward rust
and ochre trees that punctuate
a sky blue as I've ever seen it,
backdrop to flat slate roofs
and distant mountains shrugging,

If music were all I ever heard,
this wafting from Sirius 95.5
"companion radio" beside the bed:

> *love is nature's way of giving*
> *a reason to be living,*

If all I had left of my father
were hands bruised
indigo, turquoise, and magenta,
stray silver whiskers
jutting from the left nostril,
upper left lip curled upward,
and the scar on the forehead
larger than I'd remembered it,
white wingspan of moth or egret,

Would it be enough finally,
this dementia dreaming?

Hovering in Tylenol-Roxanol
half-sleep half-waking,
he dreams of delivering cakes to Harrisburg
or fists jabbing in the boxing ring
or a pretty girl walking down the street
who would become my mother.

Strains of piano and vocals
mingle with long-term memory:

> *the world stood still*
> *your fingers touched my silent heart*
> *and taught it how to sing.*

The sounds encompass us,
the past held aloft
as if he might awaken
and reenter my world
for the last time
as if it were the first.

Johnny Red

A man holds an oak leaf
as though the whole tree
grows from his hand,
the leaf-flesh reddish brown,
its extensions all thumbs.

He looks at it intently
as though it portends the future.

I can't take my eyes
off him, off his left eye,
flecked with light
like a tiny snow globe turned over.

I see just this one eye
between the leaf's jagged edges.
Leaf, hand, eye.

The man is already dying,
dying right now. I can see it in his eye.
So what? There, I have named it.
Nothing has changed.
Death is reasonable, isn't it?
Has causes, even if we dislike them?

But the story isn't death,
it's memory, the living tree,
how his nickname *Johnny Red*
once emblazoned the side
of a shiny pickup, rusted now
behind a tilted farmhouse.

When I take his palm in mine,
like a leaf, I see a satellite image
of driving directions
delineated, protruding.

Where we are going, yet unknown,
how to get there uncertain
beneath brick-red sky.

Amplification

My father sleeps
his vacant eyes ajar
until awakened

when light reenters
like an airport runway
flashing at midnight.

His breath is the shape
of things to come.
Listening, I lean left ear

toward his lips as if
toward a conch shell,
holding my breath

to amplify his world
within worlds. Sun
elongates toward evening

like a cat stretching
after a nap. Already
I miss even this.

Treatise

Brows precise, grief over-plucked.
Life feral, I sleep among cats.
They think I am one of them.

Alive in my head, my body a slow runner.
Learning yoga, extending into the crown,
I lengthen toward Krishna.

One day happy, another a swirling vortex.
Replete with contradiction,
tenant of hubris and longing.

My laughter is a train
rattling through a metropolis.
My stories, repair.

Let me know if you like words too,
if you're unafraid of sun's fierce treatise
and earth's pleated places.

Consignment Pockets

These jeans once encircled
another woman's comings and goings
known in ways I've never known
a lover or husband

the elevations and regrets
waist and thighs
betrayals and frivolity.

These are years of thrift
and vintage desire
life by consignment

scouring for what's been worn before
what's already been broken in
by love and exertion, what's sullied
but can still be scrubbed clean again.

Thrusting my hand in a pocket
I am certain I will discover
remnants of my own in its recesses

a bit of living
left for the taking.

Pressed Close to the Secrets of Water

A cupped hand cradles the conch
like a talisman or phone
that wants to be listened to
pressed whisper-close to the ear

each of us compelled to bring
the ocean home, to press close
to the secrets of water.
If I were small enough

I'd crawl inside
the shell's curvature
where someone once told me
the whole universe resides.

I'd crawl inside and dwell,
nameless, myself a tiny hatchling
reclaiming the origins
of my amphibian feet.

Temporary Vase

I scoop daylilies
into the temporary

vase of hands.
They bow just slightly

almost imperceptibly
before being plunged

into a slender pitcher
to stand devoutly

in prayer pose.
From bloom-curls

meaning escapes.
Rain scent lingers.

Whispered Season

With ghostly insistence
a possum crouches
toward morning,

feet dew-moistened,
crossing the threshold
between sleep and waking.

In these early hours
paisley-pajama'd
I rise from bed

and spy the moon
as if in a dream.
Promises *tap tap tap*

their tiny increments
of what can be reclaimed:
a half-sister, a dispatched love.

And what can't be:
childhood Augusts or first kisses.
They trail behind.

In the whispered season
the desire to do it all again
drags its tail across a canvas of grass.

Wild Articulation

Rain at last
arrives
not kind or aslant

cuts straight
to the heart
of things.

How this happens
I don't know
only that it does

air too heavy
to hold more.
Breath. Flutter.

What wants
to live
comes closer.

For a moment
held. Then
stillness.

Only so much
the soul
can take

only
prayers
of finches

whole
corrugated
sky.

Sandra Fees is a Unitarian Universalist minister who resides in Reading, Pennsylvania. She fell in love with language growing up in rural Central Pennsylvania. Her connection to poetry became deeply rooted when she studied with experimental poet John Taggart at Shippensburg University where she earned her bachelor's degree.

She also holds a master's degree from Syracuse University, where she studied creative writing, and a Master of Divinity degree from Lancaster Theological Seminary, where she is enrolled in the Doctor of Ministry program.

Formerly a poetry editor of the *Harrisburg Review*, she has had poems published in numerous journals, including *New Madrid, Touch: A Journal of Healing, Yellow Chair Review*, and FootHills Press's *Birdsong* Anthology. She has been named Berks County Poet Laureate for 2016-18.